This Book Belongs To:

____

50 SIMPLE MANDALAS

ISBN: 978-1-998058-34-1

Please visit our website for more books updates and freebies.

www.fairylandbooks.com

Printed in the USA
CPSIA information can be obtained
at www.ICGtesting.com
LVHW081928101124
796066LV00010B/194